VERONICA RUFF

A Cosy Mother's Day Table

Simple Recipes and Gentle Moments to Share

"She opens her mouth with wisdom,
and the teaching of kindness is on her tongue."

— Proverbs 31:26 (NIV)

Contents

Introduction

There is something quietly special about a table set with care.

Not for perfection, or for show, but for the simple joy of gathering. A warm cup of tea, something freshly baked, the gentle hum of conversation, and the comfort of being together.

Mother's Day can hold many emotions. For some, it is a day of celebration and gratitude. For others, it may carry longing, remembrance, or quiet reflection. Wherever you find yourself, this book has been created with you in mind.

A Cosy Mother's Day Table is not about elaborate meals or perfect presentation. It is about simple recipes, shared moments, and creating space for connection. The kind of table where stories are told, laughter is shared, and hearts feel a little lighter.

Within these pages, you will find easy, comforting recipes to enjoy at your own pace—whether you are preparing a gentle breakfast, a relaxed afternoon tea, or a simple meal shared with those you love.

At the beginning of each recipe, you will also find a short piece of Scripture. These verses are there to offer quiet encouragement and to gently remind you of love, care, and the beauty found in everyday moments.

May this book inspire you to slow down, to gather, and to create a table that feels warm, welcoming, and filled with grace.

With love,

Veronica

BREAKFAST AND BRUNCH

1. Lemonade Scones
2. Fluffy Pancakes
3. French Toast with Berries
4. Berry Breakfast Muffins (berry or apple)
5. Creamy Scrambled Eggs & Toast

Lemonade Scones

"Come to me, all you who are weary and burdened, and I will give you rest."
  — Matthew 11:28 (NIV)

There is something so comforting about warm scones fresh from the oven, shared with a cup of tea and quiet conversation.

Ingredients
   3 cups self-raising flour
   1 cup thickened cream
   1 cup lemonade (such as Sprite)
   A pinch of salt

Method
   Preheat oven to 200°C (180°C fan-forced). Line a baking tray with baking paper.
   In a large bowl, add the flour and salt. Pour in the cream and lemonade, then gently mix until just combined. Do not overmix.
   Turn the dough onto a lightly floured surface and gently bring it together. Pat it out to about 2–3 cm thick.
   Use a round cutter or glass to cut out scones and place them close together on the prepared tray.
   Bake for 12–15 minutes or until lightly golden on top.
   Serve warm with jam, and cream.

Fluffy Pancakes

"Every good and perfect gift is from above, coming down from the Father of the heavenly lights."
— James 1:17 (NIV)

Soft, golden pancakes are a simple way to make the morning feel a little more special.

Ingredients
1 cup plain flour
1 tablespoon sugar
1 teaspoon baking powder
½ teaspoon baking soda
1 cup milk
1 egg
1 tablespoon melted butter
1 teaspoon vanilla extract

Method
In a large bowl, whisk together the flour, sugar, baking powder, and baking soda.

In a separate bowl, whisk the milk, egg, melted butter, and vanilla.

Pour the wet ingredients into the dry ingredients and gently mix until just combined. Do not overmix—the batter should still be slightly lumpy.

Heat a non-stick pan over medium heat and lightly grease with butter.

Pour small amounts of batter into the pan. Cook until bubbles form on the surface, then flip and cook until golden.

Serve warm with fresh berries, maple syrup, or a dusting of icing sugar.

French Toast with Berries

Golden, lightly crisp on the outside and soft within, French toast is a simple way to turn an ordinary morning into something memorable.

Ingredients
  4 slices thick bread (such as brioche or white bread)
  2 eggs
  ½ cup milk
  1 teaspoon vanilla extract
  1 teaspoon cinnamon
  1 tablespoon butter
  To serve
  Fresh berries
  Maple syrup or honey
  A dusting of icing sugar

Method
  In a shallow bowl, whisk together the eggs, milk, vanilla, and cinnamon.
  Heat a frying pan over medium heat and add the butter.
  Dip each slice of bread into the egg mixture, allowing it to soak briefly on both sides.

Place the bread into the pan and cook until golden brown on each side.

Serve warm with fresh berries, a drizzle of maple syrup or honey, and a light dusting of icing sugar.

Berry Breakfast Muffins

"She is clothed with strength and dignity; she can laugh at the days to come."
— Proverbs 31:25 (NIV)

Soft, lightly sweet, and filled with bursts of fruit, these muffins are perfect for a gentle start to the day.

Ingredients
  2 cups self-raising flour
  ½ cup sugar
  1 cup milk
  1 egg
  ⅓ cup vegetable oil or melted butter
  1 teaspoon vanilla extract
  1 cup fresh or frozen berries (such as blueberries or mixed berries)

Method
  Preheat oven to 180°C (160°C fan-forced). Line a muffin tray with paper cases.
  In a large bowl, combine the flour and sugar.
  In a separate bowl, whisk together the milk, egg, oil, and vanilla.
  Pour the wet ingredients into the dry ingredients and gently mix until just combined. Fold in the berries.
  Spoon the mixture evenly into the muffin cases.
  Bake for 18–22 minutes or until golden and cooked through.

Allow to cool slightly before serving.

Creamy Scrambled Eggs on Toast

"Give us today our daily bread."
  — Matthew 6:11 (NIV)

Simple, warm, and nourishing, scrambled eggs on toast are a gentle way to begin the day.

Ingredients
  4 eggs
  2 tablespoons milk or cream
  1 tablespoon butter
  Salt and pepper, to taste
  2 slices bread, toasted

Method
  Crack the eggs into a bowl, add the milk or cream, and whisk gently until combined.
  Heat a non-stick pan over low heat and add the butter.
  Pour in the egg mixture and allow it to sit for a few seconds before gently stirring with a spatula.
  Continue to cook slowly, stirring gently, until the eggs are soft and creamy. Do not overcook.
  Season with salt and pepper.
  Serve immediately on warm toast.

SWEET TREATS

1. Passionfruit Melting Moments
2. Classic Vanilla Cupcakes
3. Simple Butter Cake
4. Apple Crumble Slice
5. Chocolate Brownies

Passionfruit Melting Moments

"Taste and see that the Lord is good; blessed is the one who takes refuge in him."
— Psalm 34:8 (NIV)

Light, buttery biscuits filled with a soft passionfruit cream—these are a beautiful addition to any Mother's Day table.

Ingredients
Biscuits
250g butter, softened
½ cup icing sugar
1 teaspoon vanilla extract
2 cups plain flour
½ cup cornflour

Filling
1 cup icing sugar
2 tablespoons butter, softened
1–2 tablespoons passionfruit pulp

Method
Preheat oven to 160°C (140°C fan-forced). Line baking trays with baking paper.

In a large bowl, beat the butter, icing sugar, and vanilla until light and creamy.

Add the flour and cornflour and mix until a soft dough forms.

Roll small portions of dough into balls and place onto the prepared trays. Gently flatten with a fork.

Bake for 12–15 minutes or until pale and set. Allow to cool completely.

To make the filling, mix the icing sugar, butter, and passionfruit pulp until smooth.

Sandwich two biscuits together with the filling.

Dust lightly with icing sugar if desired.

Classic Vanilla Cupcakes

"She speaks with wisdom, and faithful instruction is on her tongue."
   — Proverbs 31:26 (NIV)

Light, soft, and gently sweet, these cupcakes are a timeless treat perfect for
sharing.

Ingredients
   1 cup self-raising flour
   ½ cup sugar
   ½ cup butter, softened
   2 eggs
   1 teaspoon vanilla extract
   ¼ cup milk
   Buttercream
   1 cup icing sugar
   60g butter, softened
   1 teaspoon vanilla extract
   1–2 tablespoons milk

Method
   Preheat oven to 180°C (160°C fan-forced). Line a muffin tray with paper
cases.
   In a bowl, beat the butter and sugar until light and creamy.

Add the eggs one at a time, mixing well after each addition. Stir in the vanilla.

Fold in the flour, then add the milk and mix until smooth.

Spoon into the cases and bake for 15–18 minutes or until lightly golden.

Allow to cool completely.

For the buttercream, beat all ingredients until smooth and creamy, then spread or pipe onto the cupcakes.

Simple Butter Cake

"Give thanks to the Lord, for he is good; his love endures forever."
— Psalm 107:1 (NIV)

A soft, golden cake that feels both comforting and classic—perfect for any Mother's Day gathering.

Ingredients
1½ cups self-raising flour
¾ cup sugar
125g butter, softened
2 eggs
½ cup milk
1 teaspoon vanilla extract

Method
Preheat oven to 180°C (160°C fan-forced). Grease and line a cake tin.
In a bowl, beat the butter and sugar until light and creamy.
Add the eggs one at a time, mixing well after each addition.
Stir in the vanilla.
Fold in the flour and milk alternately, mixing until smooth.
Pour into the prepared tin and bake for 30–35 minutes or until cooked through.
Allow to cool before serving.

Apple Crumble Slice

Sweet apples with a buttery crumble topping make this slice a warm and comforting addition to the table.

Ingredients

Base
1½ cups plain flour
½ cup sugar
125g butter, melted

Filling
2 apples, peeled and sliced
2 tablespoons sugar
1 teaspoon cinnamon
Crumble
1 cup plain flour
½ cup brown sugar
75g butter

Method

Preheat oven to 180°C (160°C fan-forced). Line a baking tin.

Mix the base ingredients and press firmly into the tin.

Layer the sliced apples evenly over the base, then sprinkle with sugar and cinnamon.

For the crumble, rub the butter into the flour and brown sugar until crumbly.

Sprinkle over the apples.

Bake for 30–35 minutes or until golden.

Allow to cool before slicing.

Chocolate Brownies

"Let all that you do be done in love."
  — 1 Corinthians 16:14 (NIV)

Rich, fudgy, and deeply satisfying, these brownies are a simple way to add a little indulgence to the day.

Ingredients

200g dark chocolate
125g butter
¾ cup sugar
2 eggs
1 teaspoon vanilla extract
¾ cup plain flour

Method

Preheat oven to 180°C (160°C fan-forced). Line a square baking tin.
Melt the chocolate and butter together until smooth.
Stir in the sugar, then add the eggs one at a time, mixing well.
Add the vanilla.
Fold in the flour until just combined.
Pour into the tin and bake for 20–25 minutes or until set but still soft in the centre.
Allow to cool before slicing.

FEATURE TARTS

1. Homemade Caramel Tart
2. Lemon Tart with Fresh Cream

Homemade Caramel Tart

"The Lord is my shepherd, I lack nothing."
  — Psalm 23:1 (NIV)

Rich, smooth caramel with a simple biscuit base—this tart is a beautiful centrepiece for a Mother's Day table.

Ingredients

Base
   250g plain sweet biscuits
   125g butter, melted

Filling
   1 cup brown sugar
   100g butter
   1 can (395g) sweetened condensed milk
   2 tablespoons golden syrup
   1 teaspoon vanilla extract
   To serve
   Whipped cream

Method
Preheat oven to 180°C (160°C fan-forced).

Crush the biscuits into fine crumbs and mix with the melted butter. Press the mixture firmly into the base of a tart tin.

Bake for 10 minutes, then set aside to cool.

In a saucepan over medium heat, combine the brown sugar, butter, condensed milk, and golden syrup. Stir continuously until the mixture thickens and turns a deep caramel colour.

Remove from heat and stir in the vanilla.

Pour the caramel into the prepared base and smooth the top.

Allow to cool, then refrigerate until set.

Serve with freshly whipped cream.

Lemon Tart with Fresh Cream

"The Lord bless you and keep you;
  the Lord make his face shine on you and be gracious to you."
  — Numbers 6:24–25 (NIV)

Light, smooth, and gently sweet, this lemon tart is a refreshing addition to a
Mother's Day table.

Ingredients

Base

250g plain sweet biscuits
125g butter, melted

Filling

1 can (395g) sweetened condensed milk
½ cup fresh lemon juice
Zest of 1 lemon
To serve
Freshly whipped cream

Method

Preheat oven to 180°C (160°C fan-forced).
Crush the biscuits into fine crumbs and mix with the melted butter. Press

the mixture into the base of a tart tin.

Bake for 10 minutes, then set aside to cool slightly.

In a bowl, whisk together the condensed milk, lemon juice, and lemon zest until smooth and thickened.

Pour the filling into the prepared base and smooth the top.

Bake for 10–12 minutes until just set.

Allow to cool, then refrigerate until firm.

Serve with freshly whipped cream.

AFTERNOON TEA

1. Shortbread Biscuits
2. Jam Drops
3. Banana Bread

Shortbread Biscuits

"The Lord is good to all; he has compassion on all he has made."
  — Psalm 145:9 (NIV)

Buttery, delicate, and simple, these biscuits are perfect for a quiet moment with a cup of tea.

Ingredients
   1 cup plain flour
   ½ cup butter, softened
   ¼ cup icing sugar
   1 teaspoon vanilla extract

Method
   Preheat oven to 160°C (140°C fan-forced). Line a baking tray with baking paper.
   In a bowl, beat the butter and icing sugar until smooth and creamy.
   Add the vanilla, then gradually mix in the flour until a soft dough forms.
   Roll the dough out on a lightly floured surface and cut into shapes.
   Place onto the prepared tray and bake for 12–15 minutes or until lightly golden.
   Allow to cool before serving.

Jam Drops

Soft, buttery biscuits with a sweet centre—simple, nostalgic, and perfect for sharing.

Ingredients
   1 cup self-raising flour
   ½ cup butter, softened
   ½ cup sugar
   1 egg
   1 teaspoon vanilla extract
   Jam of choice (strawberry or raspberry works well)

Method
   Preheat oven to 180°C (160°C fan-forced). Line a baking tray with baking paper.
   In a bowl, beat the butter and sugar until light and creamy.
   Add the egg and vanilla, mixing well.
   Stir in the flour until a soft dough forms.
   Roll small portions into balls and place on the tray.
   Use your thumb or the back of a spoon to make an indent in each biscuit.
   Fill each indent with a small amount of jam.

Bake for 12–15 minutes or until lightly golden.
Allow to cool before serving.

Banana Bread

"Cast all your anxiety on him because he cares for you."
 — 1 Peter 5:7 (NIV)

Soft, moist, and gently sweet, banana bread is a comforting classic that brings warmth to any table.

Ingredients
  2 ripe bananas, mashed
  1½ cups self-raising flour
  ½ cup sugar
  1 egg
  ⅓ cup melted butter
  1 teaspoon vanilla extract

Method
  Preheat oven to 180°C (160°C fan-forced). Grease and line a loaf tin.
  In a bowl, combine the mashed bananas, egg, melted butter, and vanilla.
  Add the flour and sugar, mixing gently until just combined.
  Pour into the prepared tin and smooth the top.
  Bake for 40–45 minutes or until cooked through.
  Allow to cool slightly before slicing.

LIGHT MEALS

Simple Chicken Sandwich Filling

A light and creamy filling, perfect for simple sandwiches shared around the table.

Ingredients

2 cups cooked chicken, shredded

¼ cup mayonnaise

1 tablespoon lemon juice

Salt and pepper, to taste

Method

In a bowl, combine the shredded chicken, mayonnaise, and lemon juice.

Mix until well coated and creamy.

Season with salt and pepper to taste.

Serve in fresh bread, rolls, or sandwiches.

Egg and Mayo Sandwiches

"Give us today our daily bread."
  — Matthew 6:11 (NIV)

Simple and familiar, these sandwiches are a comforting addition to any gathering.

Ingredients
  4 eggs
  ¼ cup mayonnaise
  Salt and pepper, to taste
  Bread, to serve

Method
  Place the eggs in a saucepan and cover with water. Bring to the boil, then simmer for 8–10 minutes.
  Remove from heat, cool, and peel.
  Mash the eggs in a bowl and mix with the mayonnaise.
  Season with salt and pepper.
  Spread onto fresh bread and serve.

Easy Quiche

Warm, simple, and satisfying, this quiche is perfect for a relaxed Mother's Day meal.

Ingredients

1 sheet ready-made shortcrust pastry
4 eggs
1 cup cream
½ cup grated cheese
½ cup cooked fillings (such as ham, spinach, or vegetables)
Salt and pepper, to taste

Method

Preheat oven to 180°C (160°C fan-forced).
Line a pie or tart tin with the pastry and trim the edges.
In a bowl, whisk together the eggs and cream.
Stir in the cheese and your chosen fillings.
Season with salt and pepper.
Pour into the prepared pastry case.
Bake for 35–40 minutes or until set and golden.
Allow to cool slightly before serving.

EXTRAS AND FINISHING TOUCHES

1. Fresh Fruit Platter Ideas
2. Whipped Cream & Berry Bowl

Fresh Fruit Platter

"The Lord has done it this very day; let us rejoice today and be glad."
— Psalm 118:24 (NIV)

Fresh, colourful, and simple, a fruit platter brings brightness and balance to any table.

Ingredients

A selection of fresh fruit such as:
Strawberries
Blueberries
Grapes
Sliced melon
Kiwi fruit
Apple slices

Method
Wash and prepare all fruit.
Arrange on a large platter, mixing colours and textures for a beautiful presentation.
Serve fresh, either on its own or alongside cream or yoghurt.

Whipped Cream and Berry Bowl

"May the God of hope fill you with all joy and peace as you trust in him."
— Romans 15:13 (NIV)

Light, fresh, and gently sweet, this simple bowl is a lovely way to end a shared meal.

Ingredients
1 cup thickened cream
1–2 tablespoons icing sugar
1 teaspoon vanilla extract
Fresh berries (such as strawberries, blueberries, or raspberries)

Method
In a bowl, beat the cream, icing sugar, and vanilla until soft peaks form.
Spoon into a serving bowl and top with fresh berries.
Serve immediately.

About the Author

Veronica Ruff is an Australian author and publisher passionate about creating faith-based books that bring comfort, encouragement, and a sense of calm to everyday life.

Through her work with Integrity Press Publishing, she writes devotionals, journals, and cosy lifestyle books designed to help readers slow down, reflect, and create meaningful moments with those they love.

Her writing gently weaves together faith, home, and connection, offering simple and thoughtful ways to bring warmth and intention into daily living.

A Cosy Mother's Day Table is part of her growing collection of giftable books created to inspire connection, hospitality, and the quiet beauty of gathering around the table.

You can connect with me on:

☍ https://linktr.ee/integritypresspublishing

Also by Veronica Ruff

A Gentle Mother's Day Devotional: For Mothers, Those Who Miss Them, and Those Who Long to Be
A Gentle Mother's Day Devotional is a heartfelt 7-day journey designed to bring comfort, reflection, and quiet encouragement during the Mother's Day season.

Created for mothers, those who miss their mothers, and those who long to be, this devotional gently acknowledges the many emotions this time of year can hold-joy, gratitude, grief, and hope.

Choosing Meaningful Funeral Readings, Prayers and Hymns: A Simplified Catholic & Christian Guide for Families Making Decisions Under Pressure
When someone you love dies, decisions must often be made quickly. In the midst of grief, families are asked to choose readings, prayers and hymns that will shape a final farewell.

Choosing Meaningful Funeral Readings, Prayers and Hymns is a clear and simplified guide for Catholic and Christian families who wish to make those decisions thoughtfully, without becoming overwhelmed.

After the Funeral: A Christian Companion Guide for the First Year of Grief

A Christian Companion Guide for the First Year of Grief offers gentle reflections for those walking through the early seasons of loss. Each chapter explores experiences that many grieving people encounter during the first year, accompanied by comforting Scripture and simple prayers.

When Work Becomes War: Healing From Workplace Bullying and Betrayal

When Work Becomes War is a fierce, poetic, and unflinching testimony to the psychological toll of toxic workplaces—and to the quiet, steady power of healing and reclamation.

Drawing from lived experience, editorial clarity, and psychological insight, Veronica Ruff gives language to experiences many endure but struggle to name: gaslighting, workplace bullying, institutional betrayal, triangulation, and the systematic erosion of truth.

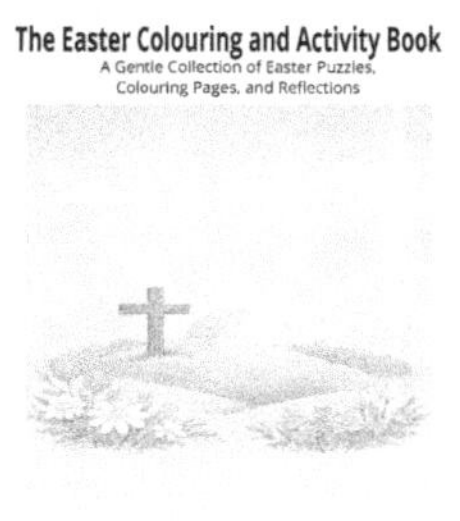

The Easter Colouring and Activity Book: A Gentle Collection of Easter Puzzles, Colouring Pages, and Reflections

The Easter Colouring and Activity Book is a gentle companion for children and families to enjoy together. Filled with simple devotionals, calming colouring pages, and thoughtful activities, this book invites moments of reflection, creativity, and connection throughout the Easter season.

The Easter Devotional: 40 Days of Prayer, Reflection and Family Devotions for Lent and Easter

A calm, family-centred devotional for Lent and Easter, designed to help parents and children slow down, reflect, and grow in faith together.

A Cosy Easter Table: Simple Recipes for Family, Friends, and Easy Hosting

A Cosy Easter Table is a warm and welcoming collection of simple recipes created for gathering with family and friends during the Easter season.